A COMMA NOT A PERIOD

A COMMA NOT A PERIOD

DONA MAY BRENNAN

Editorial Services: Karen Roberts, RQuest, LLC

Printed in the United States of America

INTRODUCTION

———

The question during different times of life is often, "What's my purpose now?" In this book I share what I discovered each time I struggled with this question. Whether it was an alarming diagnosis, deep relational disappointment, or widowhood that seemed to put a big black "period" in front of me, punctuating my struggle, God took His mercy and grace "eraser" to the period. In its place, He placed a comma, showing me that more was yet to be written. Each time he erased a period and replaced it with a comma, I discovered renewed purpose and fulfillment.

I have not written this book as a precept upon precept Bible study but instead a collection of life stories that illustrate the goodness of God in the numerous times I thought life as I had hoped was going to be completely over.

Jesus promises us newness of life. It is described as resurrection life. His resurrection life turns my disappointments and sometimes desperations into new beginnings that are fulfilling and beautiful. I pray that you will discover this simple yet transforming truth as you walk through your darker days into the light of His mercy and grace.

IN THESE PRESENT CIRCUMSTANCES

———

The memorial service for my husband of 54 years had come and gone. My loving children had settled back into their busy lives. my brother Jim called to say he was coming to visit. He had a purpose. God had impressed him with an enlightening message to give me. His timing could not have been better. I was facing my first holiday after my husband's passing.

What was the urgency of giving this message? My brother would only say what the Lord had told him to tell me. "This time in your life is not a period but simply a comma."

I laughed. I was thinking about my book, *God Is Enough for You.* It had so many commas in it that the editors said they could have made an extra chapter with just those commas!

I thought about what my brother said for months. I feel very hopeful. I am choosing to believe that God has a plan and purpose for my life, yet unfulfilled. I know that He who began a good work in me will complete it (Philippians 1:6).

What does the comma metaphor have to do with my life? It's what I'm beginning to discover.

What does it have to do with your life? Maybe my story will help you discover what it could mean for you as well.

We grow up and learn, we make decisions that change situations. Even though a trial as a child is big to us then, it is only a comma in our life. Each time of life differs from another. It does not last forever!

I once was a child with problems children face. When something bad happened, my friends and I used to say, "Let's just go eat worms." Did you ever hear that expression? Worms aren't very tasty.

Now I am a widow in my 80s with problems I must face as an adult. Do I cry out in grief, "It's all over now? I guess I will somehow just live alone until I die. Is there nothing but a big black period over my purpose for life now that I am alone? Is this the end of a meaningful life?"

Or do I choose to say, "What can I do in my new circumstance that brings freshness to hope and a new purpose?" This was not a period, an end of everything I knew and desired. It is a comma, a pause in my life with something good following.

I am learning to experience life on the other side of the commas, which can be many in our lives. My story is for anyone who has reached a place of change that felt like a big black period at the end of a sentence.

OPPORTUNITY COMMAS

———

Not long after my husband Jim passed away in 2017, opportunities came for me to go on two trips. At first I wondered, should I sit and give no effort to finding out what God has for me and just place a period here? Should I feel guilty about living my life to the fullest? Should I feel sorry for myself, looking at what I don't have or can't do with my husband? But then I saw the comma. Jim can't go on these trips, but guess what? Friends can. Family can. I can. So I went.

My 80th birthday was spent in Belize with three friends. And then I spent what would have been my 55th anniversary to Jim on board the new ship *Symphony of the Sea* cruising around Spain with six friends. The three days we had in Barcelona ministering with the homeless and sightseeing made me realize I did have more reason to live, to enjoy life, and to be a blessing to others.

In May, 2018 I went to South Dakota to be with family for my brother Mel and his wife Grada's memorial service. They had passed just one month and a day after Jim had passed. On that trip, I realized that I am now the older generation with memories I can share with their kids and grandkids.

While I was there, I visited with my brother Jim to celebrate his birthday with our families. I went to dinner with classmates, celebrating our graduation from high school in 1956. We felt like high school kids again with older bodies.

FRIENDLY COMMAS

While I am enjoying the opportunity commas God has given to me at this stage in my life, I am also realizing that people are more ready to lend a hand to a person who asks. I am now asking and receiving from others and being totally honest with them. It's a great feeling.

I am learning to let go of a few things and take up some responsibilities that my husband took care of for years. It is making me more aware of what needs to be done, how to deal with issues, and not to be shy about asking others for help.

As a new widow, I'm discovering that when I stay involved in friends lives, they are often there when I need them. When a big black period seems like it is about to hit, the love I've given others comes back just when I need it.

Who knows what the next comma will bring? Can we dream, imagine, and plan for the future even though our circumstances may change? I say YES! It doesn't matter what changes you've just been through. Start to imagine something beautiful, something good for your future.

EXCHANGE THE PERIOD

———

So what's the period in your life? Is it holding you back in some unhealthy way? What can you do about it? Only you will know the answers to those questions.

Consider some ways that could help you exchange a period to a comma.

1. Ask yourself, "What would help me get my healthy perspective and fiery passion back?"
2. Look for opportunities to stir up your faith in the future.
3. Renew healthy friendships.
4. Pray your requests.
5. Listen for answers from God's still small voice.

Answers can come through another person or something you read, hear, or see. I often pray Scriptures. The Bible has many answers and promises for a full life after a loved one is gone.

God is a good father. He wants the best for you. The enemy is the opposite. In John 10:10, we are told, *"The thief does not come except to steal, and to kill, and to destroy. I have come that they may have life and that they may have it more abundantly."*

Who will you choose to follow?

Will you let life put an early period after your name, or will you erase it in exchange for a comma?

LEARNING COMMAS

———

I have had time to ponder God's working in my life. When I thought surely life would never change, I discovered one thing I can count on—it will change!

I want to share some of what I learned along the way about God's faithful commas.

Just remember, your life is not over until God says it's over. We don't always understand the why or even the what. But if we know the Who, Jesus Christ as Lord, we won't allow periods after our names until God releases us.

Begin to fill your thought life with the study of God's love for you. Don't just read the Bible in some random reading here and there; but instead look up Scriptures on love. Think about them often. Resist thoughts of hopelessness. You are in a battle for your comma. No periods are allowed!

John 3:16 is an example. *"For God so loved the world* (YOU) *that He gave His only begotten Son, that whoever believes in Him should not perish but have everlasting life."* Get to know Jesus and think about how deeply He loves YOU!

You can also think about nature and smile at the wonder you see in its intricate beauty. How about the images of baby animals? They are so cute, innocent, and soft. I'm amazed at how God made flowers so beautiful and wildly different in design and fragrance.

I practice thinking of those things that are lovely and good because our Lord, through Paul, reminds us in Philippians 4:8 of the value of keeping our mind on these things: *"Finally, brethren, whatever things are true, whatever things are noble, whatever things are just, whatever things are pure, whatever things are lovely, whatever things are of good report, if there is any virtue and if there is anything praiseworthy-meditate on these things."*

Previously I had a battle in my mind because I veered toward the negative. During this time, I also had many struggles with health issues that added to my battle of the mind. I began reading a book about how water crystals react to music and words. Since our bodies are made up mostly of water, could it be possible that what we say, hear, and meditate on drastically changes the chemicals in our bodies? Could we have some partnership in the health of our bodies and minds by what we think, read, and listen to?

I have concluded that when we are intentional to think on the things the Bible encourages us to think about, we find yourself less inclined toward what depletes and discourages us and more toward good.

UNEXPECTED COMMAS

Sometimes God intervenes and changes the vision for our future in unexpected ways. For example, I had never thought I'd go on mission trips to other nations. I had no desire, no encouragement from my husband, and no finances of my own.

Sounds like a period, right? Enter the Holy Spirit! That period was about to change for sure.

Three friends were at dinner one night and talking about going to the Philippines to teach and help in villages. Suddenly, like a mighty wind blowing through our thinking, we were touched in a powerful way by the Holy Spirit (Acts 2:2). We knew we were to go. One of the women contacted a pastor in the Philippines to find the need for women's conferences. He cried out, "Yes! We've been praying for God to send someone to come for nine years to minister to women!"

I wondered, was God going to change my period to a comma?

The period is a place where you give up or think the circumstances will never change. Maybe you have not thought of something you desire or dream to be a possibility. The comma is a place of change, of hope, of fulfilling God's plan for your life.

I started to pray. After months of my husband saying no to this trip, he said okay, but I'd have to pay for it. When people heard I was going, they started to send money. I knew I was about to do something I'd never dreamed.

That trip was a new adventure for the entire team. Some learned to relate to others in close quarters. Some learned to have four-hour teaching classes in the outdoor heat with sweat pouring down their faces. Some ate food they would never have eaten at home. All were covered with God's presence.

When the Filipino women saw most of our team ages 60 and over were serving Jesus, they were shocked. Our children were grown, and some of us had grandchildren. Just seeing us productive and serving God gave them hope for their future. There was life after raising a family! If God could use us, He could and would use them too. Many ministries emerged from the people set free in these meetings.

Since then, many teams of women and men have gone there to teach and train. Women leaders were honored and raised up by men. Couples started and began running churches together. Thousands were giving their lives to Jesus. The other two women on that first team, Lana Heightley and Janet Mangum, have trained thousands of people in missions and are still traveling all over the world to share the Good News of Jesus.

I didn't know I'd be a part of this wonderful ministry, but then I didn't know about commas in God's plan for me either! After this trip, my husband

and my attitudes changed! The result was a very positive change for both of us.

INTERNATIONAL COMMAS

That unexpected comma led to many international commas. I was blessed to go to England and be a part of a women's conference with Pastor and Evangelist Nori Chesney where the power of God was mighty in demonstration. We'd pray and barely touch a person and they would fall down, immersed in God's presence and love. It was amazing to see and be a part of His glory being revealed to those attending the gatherings. Many were healed and set free to be all God designed for their lives.

Another time I went to England with evangelist Bunty Bunce. We went to the embassy and to the home of the ambassador from Fiji. God showed His power in answered prayer. There were instant healings, laughter, joy, and God's power setting people free from demonic attacks. It was fun. It was a comma. A comma I never expected!

So many other stories could be told about these trips, but I just want to let you know that no matter who you are or what your current circumstances, God isn't through with you yet. Step out, be available, stay teachable, and God will fill in your blanks after the comma.

The trip to Fiji was a great experience for me. One day we prayed for several politicians who were responsible to lead the country. I had a word from the Holy Spirit while asking one rather sullen looking woman if she wanted prayer. I asked her if she was in pain in her back area. She brightened up and said her sciatic nerve was so painful she was bedridden at times. I laid hands on the area, and God instantly healed her! This woman then got up from her chair, took the microphone, and stated in a matter-of-fact voice, "God just healed me."

One woman there was employed by United Nations and ended up being baptized with her husband and daughter in the ocean. They have been serving Jesus ever since.

We took part in conferences with each of us on our team taking individual groups aside for teaching. I taught on unequally yoked marriages. Women were weeping and wanting to hug me as they left. They felt someone understood them for the first time.

I discovered that few people understand how very difficult life is for Christian women there. Some are abused by husbands because they believe in Jesus. Loneliness, oppression, and fear are daily companions. A hug from someone who understands and cares is desperately needed. In exchange, I received their love gratefully because we were all in the same circumstance in varying degrees.

On these trips, I learned that people in some countries seem to be able to identify demon activity when they see it more readily than others. They long for freedom from these evil spirits. As we ministered the power of the name of Jesus, they were delivered.

In the four gospels and in the New Testament church, setting people free from the evil spirits was practiced. Jesus commissioned the disciples to go out on their first training trip with this command: *"And as you go, preach, saying, 'The kingdom of heaven is at hand.' Heal the sick, cleanse the lepers, raise the dead, cast out demons. Freely you have received, freely give"* (Matthew 10:7-8).

He also said to them, *"Behold, I give you the authority to trample on serpents and scorpions, and over all the power of the enemy, and nothing shall by any means hurt you"* (Luke 10:19).

The disciples' lives would never be the same again. This comma (new direction) began their times of sharing the Good News of Jesus as they traveled. They demonstrated God's love and power to their world. They didn't stop until God put a period at the end of their lives. (Yes, even martyrdom was part of the disciples' destiny.)

On the next trip to the Philippines, our team preached in churches and prayed for lines of people to be healed. We were delighted to hear that a large number were instantly healed. Some saw limbs grow back, and many legs straightened to the length of the other leg. We read the miracles in the book of Acts in the Bible, and we saw it in person. Hearing was restored and pain left backs.

Japan was an amazing and life-changing adventure. The percentage of Christians in Japan is small. Believers are open to learn and share their faith, and I was honored to be with them.

I was so thankful to have my friend Rocky lead me by the hand through the complex train stations. She was born there and ministers in America to Japanese women. Coming from a Buddhist background, Rocky accepted the Lord in America. After prayer, her sister in Japan was healed of a painful physical ailment. Her transformation was evident to all as she became God's child as well.

Being a Buddhist was not a period in Rocky's life; it was a comma. She can relate her experiences to minister the life and love of Jesus to Buddhists in effective ways.

No matter how you were taught to believe, the truth of Jesus being our Lord and Savior is powerful! God changes your periods into wonderful, life-giving commas. He gives you life abundantly as you lean on Him in your devastating challenges. It begins by repenting, turning around, and living in His love and forgiveness. Ask Jesus to forgive you of sin and accept His gift of eternal life as your own. You can do it right now. Join the family of God. I want to spend eternity with you, so ask Him now!

TEACHING COMMAS

I really felt unqualified to go places and speak to anyone before I experienced the power of the love of God and His enabling Spirit. What would I have to say? Then I remembered that when the Holy Spirit lives inside of a person, He brings to mind what they are to say. John 14:26 says, *"But the Helper, the Holy Spirit, whom the Father will send in My name, He will teach you all things, and bring to your remembrance all things that I said to you."*

When I heard the words coming out of my mouth, I was amazed at the wisdom and love I had the privilege to share. It was a true high!

Do you want this high and holy life? Turn to Jesus. Get to know Him by reading the Bible and studying with groups of like-minded people. Talk to Him and pray with others of like faith. You will experience how wonderful it is to be a part of answered prayer!

Don't wait on others. Make the first move! Accept His holy period to any ungodly decisions or actions in your past. He will remove the limiting periods. Welcome His comma into your new life.

FAMILY COMMAS

At a much earlier time in my life, as a young married woman, I thought my life was a period with no possible change. My husband and I wanted another child after the first two were in grade school. The doctors informed me that it was highly unlikely.

I started going to a Bible study. Someone there told me that I could ask God what I should do with my excess time. I questioned doing it at first, but what could it hurt? I prayed, "Lord, what should I do about my time now that the girls are in school? Oh yes, and please give me a sign!"

You've probably figured out that I got pregnant the next month. So was the period regarding the size of my family permanent? No, because God gave me my heart's desire.

Don't give up when you don't see your prayer answered right when you ask. Hold on to your faith and keep thanking God for the answers. And don't put time limits on what you asked for either. Let God determine the boundaries of yes and no. You can relax and just keep living for Him and know God loves you and wants the best for you.

I experienced another family comma later on when my mother became gravely ill. *What clothes should pack for the funeral,* I wondered. God had other plans.

The traveling minister that had led my parents to salvation years earlier in South Dakota had written a booklet, and a woman I met at church from Texas gave it to me to read. I didn't know the writer was the evangelist that my mom so admired, but I sent the booklet to her in the hospital at a very dangerous time in her sickness. She was thrilled and read it off and on that night. The next day, she was well and went home!

When I talked to her by phone, she said she saw the author's picture, recognized him and read all the healing Scriptures in the booklet that night. At the time of her salvation years before, he had prayed for her healing. She was healed of diabetes.

Whatever it takes to change our periods into commas, God will use. I can just see Him smiling. My mom lived until age 95. The outfit I was going to wear to her funeral didn't fit thirty years later!

I have so many stories I could share from my walk with Jesus. He means so much to me. Even if He didn't delight me in surprising me with answers to prayer, He would still be everything to me. Sometimes I receive just what I ask for. Other times, I am the answer to someone else's prayer. What does it matter as long as I have the honor of serving the God of the universe in a personal way?

For years I longed for my husband to share my faith and these experiences with God. Sometimes I wondered what could be wrong with me because he didn't want what meant so much to me On and on I'd think and ponder the why.

One day I had lunch with two godly women who were casual acquaintances. Out of the blue one said, "I really feel that you are the answer to two women's prayers." That got my attention. I was ready for a good laugh or a deep sense of fulfillment. But to my amazement, she said the women had prayed for my husband many years ago that God would give him a godly wife to show him His love.

Well, that information ceased to be funny. I didn't like it one bit. I thought, why should I have been chosen for this privilege? I'd rather be married to a follower of Jesus and certainly an easier man to live with than my husband.

On reflection, I'm reminded of the words In John 15:13 that say that no greater love has a person than to lay their life down for others. Back then I felt that I had certainly laid down mine by staying with this man. So if that was to be one of my greatest ministries on earth, so be it. I decided to learn to praise God, accept His will, and rejoice, trusting God.

God was so faithful to make Himself real to Jim. At the end of his life, he made a commitment to Jesus! Luke 15:7, 10 says that the angels rejoice over one sinner who repents! What I thought was a period turned into commas of joy and forgiveness. We will have all of eternity to fellowship and enjoy one another.

IDEA COMMAS

———

After Jim went to heaven. I asked the Lord what I should do. My family didn't live in California. I asked Him to be specific. If I was to move from California away from all my lifetime friends, I said that I wanted to sell my house without a realtor. I even had the faith to ask that buyers would come to my door and accept my price without negotiation. Within a week, my requests were answered.

I moved to Indiana where most of my family lived. As it turns out, moving to Indiana was just another pause, a time to get a new mindset, have new adventures and goals, expect new friends, and write new books. This verse of Scripture has guided me in my new life: *"A man who has friends must himself be friendly; but there is a friend who sticks closer than a brother"* (Proverbs 18:24).

I've taken my time meeting people as opportunities arise. I go to dinner with widows in the neighborhood. I go to water aerobics several times a week to meet others. I leave my garage door open so neighbors will know I'm home and friendly. I joined a regular women's Bible study. I started going to church with one of my family members nearby. I am slowly meeting people in the church. A lovely neighbor reached out to me immediately and made it easier to settle into a new area. She has become a good friend.

These opportunities would never have happened if I hadn't stepped out and made myself available. I realized that friends come in most cases after I've reached out.

I want to encourage you, the reader, that life is constantly changing. It's your choice to look forward to the new. Perhaps the best is yet to come! We have a choice of what to believe and what to do, so why not expect something good? Enjoy the good memories and forget the bad ones. Remember that heaven is our eternal reward and peace!

We all have problems, but we also have the opportunity to ask God for wisdom. Find Scriptures that tell us to ask, seek and knock. Learn to identify His leading by listening to what seems like a small voice inside and by remaining teachable.

COMMA KISSES

———

Sometimes God answers our prayers before we ask (Isaiah 65:24). I often think of these answers as kisses from the Father.

My daughter Cynthia was looking for a full-time teaching job after being a stay-at-home mother for years. She had taught full time for over ten years before having children, but now nothing but part-time jobs were available. She prayed and waited, applying for jobs all over.

It's a hard time when you can't find the position you want. It looks very much like a period is firmly in place. Discouragement sets in. How could you ever be the one offered the job?

Just when Cynthia was ready to call and accept a part-time job offer, the phone rang. It was a principal from a school where she had not applied, and he didn't know her. Cynthia was offered a full-time teaching position sight unseen! The job had become available on the spur of the moment. A worker in the office knew Cynthia and recommended her. Who but God could have arranged that?

Need a job? This story isn't the way jobs are normally given to people, but when God wants to put a comma in a person's life, nothing can stop

Him. Pray, have faith in Him, walk in peace, and be ready to be an excellent employee when the job opens.

When things feel like they will never change and you think all of this teaching sounds okay for me but you have tried everything and it looks like a period every day, put your circumstances in the Lord's hands (Psalms 31:15). He will move on behalf of the faith of your prayers. He is faithful. He knows how to get people to the place of accepting His love and salvation and we don't. Treat this time with a comma, and it will change sooner or later.

In my teens, I wanted to go to Bible college. I found one several towns away from our farm. My youth group went to visit. I was impressed with the level of the students' Bible knowledge. It created a hunger inside of me to know more about God's Word. I wanted to go there after I graduated from high school.

I asked my dad about it, and he promptly said no. He thought I should be happy that he'd allowed me to go to high school. He said I should look for a husband, preferably a farmer, and be like his mother, sisters, and wife. He thought I'd be happy in this role.

I was very sad when this period was placed on my dream. I didn't think about it again and actually forgot about it as I made decisions for my life. I didn't want to get married then, and I didn't want to be a farmer's wife, so I made other decisions, with some mistakes along my single way, until I married at age twenty-five to a city boy. I found out life could be hard in the suburbs as well as on a farm! That was a rude awakening.

God was not stopped by a period someone else had placed in my life. Forty years later, a friend said she heard about a Bible school opening up one night a week for adult students. My heart went wild with hope. I didn't have the money, but one night a week was something I might manage.

Out of the blue, an acquaintance asked me to go in with her in selling personalized purses and small luggage items sold at home parties. She said we would make enough money from the first party to pay for a kit. After the kit was ordered, she backed out.

Those circumstances made a way that I wouldn't have taken alone to have a small business and eventually earn enough money to pay for two years of Bible school. I reclaimed my desire from years before. Psalm 37:4 says, *"Delight yourself also in the Lord, and He shall give you the desires of your heart."* God took the period my dad had put in my life and turned it into a comma!

I hope you realize that just because something seems out of reach at the time, it may just be for that time. Start to dream, find a way to go for your desire, and keep thanking our Father God that He alone can make all things work out for good (Romans 8:28).

Just as the Lord uses people to bring your dreams into reality, the enemy uses people to try to bury them. God wants to give you an abundant life, and part of it is the fulfillment of dreams and desires

He put within you. Maybe your long-ago wishes are able to come to pass in this time of your life. Dig them up and start planning for new purposes.

TIMING COMMAS

———

I read about a woman in her 80s who had always wanted to go to college and decided to do it. She became friends with so many young students, becoming a grandmother to all. She loved on them and took time with each one, and she graduated with many joyous cheers. Her dream was fulfilled at last. Months later she went to be with her Jesus in heaven, leaving behind a legacy for those students.

This woman's dream happened because she stepped out and decided to do something new. Her age didn't dictate a period. Instead, she chose to leave this world with a comma in her legacy.

I am asking God what I should do now. In the meantime, I am putting my hand to what I can do before me. As I look back at my life, I can see where I missed filling empty places at times by thinking circumstances had to be the way I thought they should be with no variation. It's not too late for another comma.

DIRECTION COMMAS

———

I n my 60's, my husband and I moved to an area some distance away from friends, church, and the familiar and comfortable settings we once had. I had been a leader in my church for the women ministry and wanted to find a place to serve, so I immediately began looking for a new church home. I met with a wonderful pastor of a church and offered to teach classes for both men and women, bringing my education and experience into the teaching.

The pastor and I had a difference of opinion on one subject. I put a period down and went to another church, then another one. It seemed as if I never really fit in anywhere. I was lonely, sticking to my belief system that others had to agree with everything I believed even some things were not core issues in the kingdom of God. It was hurtful and became very limiting.

Sometimes answers are right in front of us. God doesn't always answer the way we think He should.

After twelve years, my husband and I we moved again to a different area to retire. This time I realized I could fulfill God's call on my life if I just relaxed and loved others. I began attending a church similar to the one I refused to go to years ago and found it a fulfilling and enjoyable place to serve. I stopped expecting the people there to do everything the way I would want it done. Instead I went humbly praying and genuinely hoping I could bring wisdom and love to the younger generation and enjoy fellowship with the older ones.

I joined a local women's Bible study and gained a new family that I loved. I went to another neighborhood Bible study and had the freedom to share anything the Lord inspired me to say. Finally I let God take the period off and place His comma there. I'm living the "after period" life.

CONNECTION COMMAS

———

Some of my life choices brought pain I didn't need to go through. I've learned that we can lean on the Lord, listen to His leading as we move forward in faith, and see good things happen to us. I've learned to follow the peaceful road open before me.

Some of you may have made choices that brought you pain as well. Some have been left by a husband or boyfriend with the children and have little support. You are facing a very difficult time in your life. Your choices affect both you and your kids. During such times, isolation can be a problem. People don't know what you need if you are not among them and at least partially open to them. Read your Bible and connect with other believers. When you need comfort, help, or advice, let them know where you are struggling. You will find people reaching out to you in comfort and help.

You are not alone, and this is not a period. It is a comma. You will look back someday at this time, realizing how important your choices were to you and your children. You will grow up spiritually in the hard times. You will find strength you never knew you had. You will learn to lean on God because He is your help. God is your ultimate help, wisdom, and love.

It's best not to let only one person speak into your life. The Bible tells us in Proverbs 11:14 that there is safety in a multitude of counselors. Go and seek people of wisdom and victory in their lives. Before making choices, verify your steps with Scripture and prayer.

If your choices are tormenting you or if the choices of others are hurting you, it is not the end but a pause. These words of a song are a reminder: "Something beautiful, something good, all my confusion He understood. All I had to offer Him was brokenness and strife. And He made something beautiful out of my life." Let the Lord Jesus make something beautiful out of the rest of your life.

When my girls were young, I often wondered if the hopes and dreams I had for my own life were over. I loved being a mom, but I didn't have the love and support I needed from my husband. I felt trapped. I thought and thought of how I could get out of the hopelessness I felt. I wanted a choice that would be life changing.

One day I went to see about getting a divorce, but the Holy Spirit spoke almost audibly. "Did I tell you to do this?" The answer was no, and I went back home.

I'm sharing this personal information so you know you are not alone in your pain, whatever it is. I also want you to know that God will bless your obedience beyond anything you ever dreamed. He is a good Father, and He loves you, plans to bless you. Change will take dedication and time, but if you endure, many blessings will come to you.

DO AND DON'T COMMAS

Let these thoughts inform your choices.

- Don't immediately say that whatever it is can't happen for you.
- Don't listen to all the reasons why I did what I did because they won't work for you.
- Don't say you've tried and God didn't come through.
- Do say what you desire and find Scriptures with promises to build your faith.
- Do pray them over your situation.

Romans 2:11 (NIV) says, *"For God does not show favoritism."* I am comforted by the song that declares, "What He has done for others, He'll do for you. With arms wide open, He'll pardon you. It is no secret, what God can do."

I sing the doxology often. "Praise God from whom all blessings flow. Praise Him all creatures here below. Praise him above ye heavenly host. Praise Father, Son, and Holy Ghost." It brought me closer to the Lord always making me feel good. I sing this song over and over, searching to praise my Savior with a pure heart. As I do, I find myself feeling that I just can't thank Jesus enough.

I know He loves it when we think of Him, singing praises and just saying, "I don't know what to do, Father. Help me!" He is pleased with us when we love Him and others, sharing our joy and concerns with Him. He is our loving Father. I know one day I'll be in that heavenly choir praising Jesus with all of my being. Until then, I feel the limitations we feel while in this world.

In my spirit, I can be in the huge group of worshipers described in Psalms 150, and you can too. Here are the words:

Praise the Lord!
Praise God in His sanctuary;
Praise Him in His mighty firmament!
Praise Him for His mighty acts;
Praise Him according to His excellent greatness!
Praise Him with the sound of the trumpet;
Praise Him with the lute and harp!
Praise Him with the timbrel and dance;
Praise Him with stringed instruments and flutes!
Praise Him with loud cymbals;
Praise Him with clashing cymbals!
Let everything that has breath praise the Lord.
Praise the Lord!

HEALTH COMMAS

M any times in my life health was a big factor to what I was able to do. There were times when a period could have ended my life. My childhood was riddled with sickness. Every childhood disease threatened my life. I remember almost drowning, and I battled cancer for years.

Each of these challenges would bring me to a critical place, but God turned each one into a comma.

No one in my family knew how to find peace of mind. None knew to tell me that Jesus bore my sins and took a whipping for my healing and my peace of mind. As an adult, I was so excited to read these words in the Bible: *"But He was wounded for our transgressions. He was bruised for our iniquities; the chastisement for our peace was upon Him. and by His stripes we are healed"* (Isaiah 53:5). My faith was ignited to believe in God's Word and expect healing.

During the years 1970 to1984, I lived a life of joyful answers to prayer for myself and for others. I had no doubt that God would heal me every time I had a test. I rejoiced at the chance to let God prove Himself. It was an exciting way to live.

After those years, I mistakenly thought I would never have to go through any of those trials again. Then all hell seem to come against me at one time. At first I rejoiced, then little doubts started as I grew weaker. I endured many tormenting thoughts. Little did I know my outlook would change bit by bit.

Finally I did what I thought I had to do medically. I learned that God uses many ways to heal. That understanding really helped me in future decisions.

It's been fifty-four years since then, and yet I have never had a "free from cancer" report. But I am alive and healthy. God honored my unbelief, my weak prayers, my desperate cry. He took away the period and put a lovely comma there instead.

I'm praising Him for His wondrous acts, and you can too!

SEASON COMMAS

S easons of loneliness come to everyone. Seasons of understanding self-worth are important. Seasons of joy and friendship make life special. Knowing we can be a part of bringing encouraging days to others is a good season.

Our measuring stick for the seasons in our life is God's Word, the Bible. In every season, we can have the joy of knowing we are God's friend. These words encourage me: *"You are My friends if you do whatever I command you. No longer do I call you servants for a servant does not know what his master is doing; but I have called you friends, for all things that I hear from My Father I have made known to you"* (John 15:14-15).

SUFFERING COMMAS

A s I sat by my husband's bed in the hospital near the end of his life, I tried to take one day at a time. Only God knows the future, I told myself. He knows every one of our days from beginning to end.

I reflected on these words: *"I will praise You, for I am fearfully and wonderfully made; Marvelous are Your works, And that my soul knows very well. My frame was not hidden from You, When I was made in secret, And skillfully wrought in the lowest parts of the earth. Your eyes saw my substance, being yet unformed. And in Your book they all were written, The days fashioned for me, When as yet there were none of them. How precious also are Your thoughts to me, O God! How great is the sum of them"* (Psalms 139:14-17).

I desired to become loving, kind, and patient, enduring with joy and peace throughout it all. I deeply wanted that desire for my husband too.

For nine months, he suffered medical procedures with pain and anger. For fifty-plus years, many people had prayed for him to find his peace with Jesus. He struggled with doubt. He blamed it on what he perceived Christians saying or doing that he thought was ridiculous. At times he fought very hard to convince me and the girls that we were living in a make-believe world. He thought that if there was a God, He didn't care much about people in a real way.

That thinking happens when we focus on people and not on God in our life. The Bible tells us that if we seek Him, we will find Him (Deuteronomy 4:29, I Chronicles 16:10, Psalms 9:9-10, Romans 10:13, Jeremiah 29:13).

There Jim was, with time ticking away, trying not to think or talk about eternity. He wondered what the good was of all the prayers for his healing. I knew that God had a perfect plan, but it was hard to see any reason for this trial in those stressful moments.

One day Jim asked me if I was working too hard. Why was I so tired? I said "No, I'm not physically tired, but I am emotionally tired because I don't know, when you die, if you will go to heaven." He assured me that he was going to heaven. I saw no evidence of him wanting to pray, see a priest or pastor, or talk about God or life after death. It was so hard for me. It must have been hard for him as well.

After many trips to ER, we had no idea that the trip he made on September 27 would be his final one to the hospital. After he was given oxygen, and he called me for the last time and was happy to tell me that all he needed was an oxygen machine at home, just like he'd been telling everyone. The hospital, however, had decided to admit him.

I knew that I couldn't take care of him alone at home anymore, so I'd already contacted so our daughter Kathleen from Indiana to come to help. She was scheduled to arrive the next day.

Early in the morning that next day, September 30, 2017, I received a phone call from ICU. Jim was having trouble breathing. Our daughter Cynthia went with me to the hospital about 8 a.m. At the ICU, we put on the required gowns and masks to be with him. Not long after our arrival, a nurse came and asked Jim if he wanted life support. He asked her what the bottom line was. She told us all then that he had only from an hour to a day to live.

We had never been told anything like that in all the months Jim had been to doctors. We went into shock. It was a now-or-never time. Would Jim let God into his heart, give God his life?

These Scriptures came to my mind.

"For God so loved the world that He gave His only begotten Son, that whoever believes in Him should not perish but have everlasting life" (John 3:16).

"If we confess our sins, He is faithful and just to forgive us our sins and to cleanse us from all unrighteousness" (1 John 1:9).

Jim said he wanted to see a priest, and then he made his choice to go to heaven and receive the peace of God that passes understanding. It was a miracle to all who had prayed over half a century for that moment to happen.

Stephanie, our youngest child who lives in Indiana, miraculously made it to the hospital 20 minutes before her father died. As soon as her sister Cynthia had called her earlier in the day, she rushed to the airport in Indianapolis. A woman there helped her find the best option, an upcoming flight going to Ontario, California. She would have to rent a car there and drive to Orange County on crowded freeways. The woman got her onto the already fully booked plane. One seat was available in the front row of the plane.

On the way to the gate, Stephanie stopped for a coffee, and the server told her she wouldn't take any money. She told Stephanie that the Lord told her to give it to her!

The plane landed at the first stop, where some passengers were to change planes. When the door of the plane opened, a man said, "Stephanie Dennis, follow me." She was rushed to a gate where a plane had waited 45 minutes for her with one seat open, and it was in the front row again. The plane was not going to Ontario but John Wayne airport in Orange County, 10 ten minutes from the hospital.

Coincidence? Or God showing His loving hand!

All three girls were with Jim, singing, when he looked up with eyes shining, smiled, and left his body. His comma was in place, and he was in the presence of his Father God and loved ones. What a day of rejoicing for him and for us. A miracle of salvation had taken place after many years of the girls and me fearing he would not be with us forever.

That was not the end of this story. To get a date for the service and a place to hold the celebration of life for the eleven grandchildren, nine from Indiana, as well as Stephanie's husband Donovan and a nephew from South Dakota, seemed impossible. Some had work, some had school. The only day everyone could be there was a Saturday, six days later.

Travel arrangements were made, and places for everyone to stay as well as food for them were provided. A place for the service was secured (the only day available was the day everyone could attend). Arrangements were also made for a boat to take his ashes to the ocean, as he had requested.

The boat excursion itself was a miracle. We left early on a boat that had been fully booked for that day. The captain had made a deal with us to go earlier than his first booking.

At a moment of quiet peace, Kathleen sang the song, *Love Lifted Me.* Do you know the lyrics? "I was sinking deep in sin, far from the peaceful shore. Very deeply stained within, sinking to rise no more. But the Master of the Sea heard my despairing cry. From the waters lifted me, now safe am I. Love lifted me, love lifted me. When nothing else could help, love lifted me." It was as if we could feel the love of Jesus lifting Jim up to Himself.

The release of his ashes was a wonderful send off for everyone. We shared about Jim's life with funny and touching stories. Knowing we would see him again in heaven was comforting. We felt God's presence in a powerful way on that boat!

Another wonderful happening on the boat was when Stephanie came over to me and gave me a pendant from her necklace. She said, "God told me to give this to you. It is a symbol of all the pain and longing you experienced with Dad. As you throw it into the ocean, all unforgiveness, anger, and resentment will be buried with his ashes, and you will be free." What a gift. I have not had one problem with any of those feelings since then.

What can I say to the faithfulness of a God that is definitely involved in our lives and loves us so much? Even death is not a period. It is a comma for all those who belong to Christ. Thank you, Lord, for commas!

GROWING COMMAS

Wе never stop growing! Here are a few more insights from my life that may relate to your life as well.

I became a grandmother in my middle 50's for the first time. How exciting! Then grandchildren started to come regularly, and each one was very special. I assumed I'd go on having little ones to play with and be a part of their life.

I am constantly amazed at this time in my life that the older grandchildren have married and started their own families. My youngest grandchild is now a teenager, and I have my first great granddaughters. Children are not a period. Grandkids are not a period. Great grandchildren won't be a period either. They are little commas in life. What a wonderful way to look at a growing family.

I know that my children are blessed (Psalms 112:2). No matter what version of this Scripture I read, the idea is that my offspring will be blessed with God's love and find fulfillment. Whatever happens to them is a comma, not a period.

If you are weary praying for your children, read verses about Gods heart for children. Don't give up hope. Don't put a period after your children's names! Whatever they say or do, remember, it's only a comma. A brief time until change comes. Speak what you desire them to be, not what you see in them in the present. Your faith will develop if you regularly speak good into their lives.

When Gabriel, my youngest grandchild, was little, he was constantly smiling, talking and building something. I couldn't understand half of what he was talking about, but I enjoyed his enthusiasm and his joy at sharing what he loved to do. I could have learned more about action figures, Legos, and the books he devoured, but I didn't. Do I do the same thing with God? Maybe I need to get more serious about learning God's language of love. How about you?

I wear glasses to read, which may surprise you as I'm only 80ish. When print is smaller and is in a lighter shade of black, if I hold the print closer to my eyes and put more effort into seeing it, I see it better. Likewise, as I hold God's Word closer and become more intent on what it says, putting more effort into understanding it, my relationship with Jesus and a fuller understanding of His love grow. I may read something I already knew or something I never realized before. No matter what I read, it's always amazing.

SOUP AND SALAD COMMAS

—

I f you know me, you know I am not interested in cooking. I cook as we all do, but more out of need than enjoyment. My best concoctions are soup and salads. Everything goes into both except the cat.

Lettuce for salads, all kinds of veggies, nuts, fruit, tuna or chicken, leftovers, crunchy goodies, and whatever else my hand finds goes into the salad. The same idea with soup. It is somewhat like our walk with Jesus. He is doing the cooking. Our job is to be confident in His outcome.

Philippians 1:6 says, *"Being confident of this very thing, that He who has begun a good work in you will complete it until the day of Jesus Christ."*

1 Peter 1:6-7 says, *"In this (faith for salvation) you greatly rejoice, though now for a little while, if need be, you have been grieved by various trials, that the genuineness of your faith, being much more precious than gold that perishes, though it is tested by fire (like my simmering soup) may be found to praise, honor, and glory at the revelation of Jesus Christ."*

You get the point. Sometimes we "simmer" for years. We think God has put a period in our life and nothing will ever change or get better. But He is allowing time to bring out the best flavors in us. We are to be a sweet-smelling aroma to the Lord, as described in these words: *"Now thanks be to God who always leads us in triumph in Christ, and through us diffuses the fragrance of His knowledge in every place. For we are to God the fragrance of Christ among those who are being saved and among those who are perishing. To the one we are the aroma of death, leading to death, and to the other the aroma of life leading to life. And who is sufficient for these things?"* (2 Corinthians 2:14-15).

Even as we "cool off," God is not done with us and can heat us up again in His time. Soup smells so good as it is simmering! We smell so good to God when in the hard times we hold tight to Him.

The salad of our life starts with a base of lettuce, or salvation in our story. God adds the fruit of the Spirit, which is love, peace, joy, patience, self-control, longsuffering, gentleness, and kindness (Galatians 5:22-23). Each item enriches our lives. He spices up our faith by filling us with the Holy Spirit. He makes even sour things and hurtful things taste good when covered with His presence.

ARTFUL COMMAS

—

Monet, the famous impressionist painter in Europe, painted the same lily pond hundreds of times. As his eyesight failed in later years, he painted large murals filled with lilies and ponds and people he had painted so many times. Diminished eyesight could have been a period in his life, but he made it into a comma and adjusted. You may once have been excited about something or someone, but with time or change of circumstances, the interest, excitement, and meaning diminished. Period? Or comma?

Sometimes when I read the Bible, I read something that just fits my need and I'm thrilled. Later when I read the same Scriptures, they may not have the same effect and that's okay. As I continue to put God's Word into me, however, I gain other insights, and more pieces of the puzzle of life fall into place so I can share them with others. What I share may help them know that where they are in their life is just a comma for now, not a period.

Life has more than one path of purpose. Joy or discouragement is dependent upon how you look at your circumstances. Is the glass half full or half empty right now for you? Keep a healthy perspective in every season of your life, during each trial and each blessing. Always remember that God loves you!

BIBLE STORY COMMAS

———

I have meditated on the lives of some of people in the Bible who may have thought that what they were going through was the end of hope, dreams, or the possibility of change.

Think about Moses, for example, when he was 40 years old, an educated son of the Pharaoh's daughter. He killed an Egyptian man and ran away in fear. His next 40 years were spent as a sheep herder in the desert. Did he think of all the comfort and privileges he had left behind? Did he think living in the desert would be his life forever?

Forty years is a long time. The Bible implies that during those 40 years, he lost his confidence as a leader, his speech ability, and his identity in Egypt. He wasn't living the life of an Israelite or Egyptian, but instead a common sheep herder. Did Moses see that time as the end of anything better or new? Can you relate?

Sometimes even when we start out with love, direction, and good intentions, we find ourselves in situations that are very difficult. Do we just give up and think God put a period in our life, meaning no change, hope gone, and dreams disintegrating? We don't always understand the reasons, but we can view our circumstances as a comma, a pause that will eventually bring about change.

Moses was working as a typical shepherd on a typical day in the desert, watching the sheep, when he saw a strange scene that caught his attention. A bush was on fire but not burning up. He had no idea how much his life was about to change as he investigated.

On a day when you are working at your regular job or engaged in the routine things of life, God may break in and turn your period into a new adventure.

Moses heard a voice speaking to him from the fire, and he knew it was God. An impossible task was put before him to accomplish. He was to lead millions of people out of slavery and into the land God had promised them 400 years before. But Moses had no confidence at that point. He was afraid to go back to Egypt. He didn't like crowds, attention, and especially responsibility. He had a list of reasons why he couldn't do what God asked him to do. After arguing with God, Moses was obedient to God. Read about all the miracles God then performed through Moses (see Exodus 14).

It's okay to question God. He can take it! Just be sure to obey Him, regardless of how you see yourself or your circumstances. Step out of your period (hopelessness) in life into the comma (new things) God offers. It may be difficult looking to Him and not to your own abilities or desires, but consider what He did for Moses and be encouraged (Romans 2:11, Acts 10:34)

.God loved Moses and talked with him face to face. Deuteronomy chapter 34 tells about the end of Moses' life. Joshua was the one God picked to go on into the Promised Land to finish the work Moses had begun. Joshua had been trained by Moses and had learned to listen to God for himself. Sometimes we are the ones God chooses to start something, but someone else is sometimes sent to continue or finish or it.

From the age of 80 to 120, Moses led millions of people through the desert. He was a judge, spiritual leader, and more. He had his eyesight and strength to complete his task, but only listening to God could keep him strong and make him victorious. The same was true of Joshua. He followed God all of his life, taking back land from enemies and dividing it among the tribes as instructed.

Another character whose life I have meditated on is Joseph, son of Jacob the patriarch. He was loved and treated special by his father. His brothers were jealous of him to the point of selling him into slavery when he was a young man. Did Joseph see his years of slavery and years in prison as a period in his life? He must have had a relationship with God that grew and matured throughout the years. He did everything with excellence, and as far as we can tell by the story, he did not became bitter or give up.

Joseph's life is a good example for us in difficult circumstances. Even if circumstances seem unchangeable, we can grow into mature and wise people. Our growth is not dependent on others or our situation but on our relationship with God.

I doubt Joseph thought he would he would end up second in command of ruling Egypt. Moses probably never thought he was going to be appointed to lead the Israelites out of slavery. Take heart, because God has a plan for your life, and He will bring it to pass in the right time.

We have different distractions and trials than Moses and Joshua, but we are here to take the land back from the devil's influence. We can get distracted by everyday problems. but like the people of old, we can choose to be directed by God, walking on with Him no matter what life looks like.

What plans do you suppose God has for you? Is anything too hard for Him? Can you start to hope and believe that God is a good God and His plans for you are for good and not evil? *"For I know the thoughts that I think toward you, says the Lord, thoughts of peace and not evil, to give you a future and a hope"* (Jeremiah 29:11). Read the next two verses,12 and 13, and be encouraged.

Joseph died at the age of 110. God had prepared him for his destiny, which Joseph fulfilled in excellence. I imagine God saying, *"Well done, good and faithful servant"* (Matthew 25:23) at the end of his life.

I could give you many more examples of people

in the Bible, including those Jesus met, whose lives were changed in different ways. Why don't you start researching these stories in the Bible for yourself?

Here's what you will discover. Even if you haven't been faithful your whole life to God, a comma is there just waiting for you to add to your story. As you reach out and get to know Jesus better and seek what He wants you to be, get ready for a new adventure!

AN OPEN-ENDED SENTENCE

———

I am at that place in my life where I am not sure what I am to do next. I was a wife for over fifty years, and now I'm a widow. I raised my family the best I knew how, and now I am a great grandmother.

Can I relax and just live one day at a time, knowing that God has a plan for my so-called golden years, or should I sit back, feeling bad because many of the things or people that brought me joy are gone? Should I try new things or continue the old ways of thinking and just sit down, waiting to die? It is my choice.

So I choose to see myself as complete in Jesus, ready for more of His adventures. I embrace new friendships and reach out to others by a phone call, text, or card. I stay in touch with older friends as well. It's such a delight to have people I care for returning love to me. It feels good to be a comma of hope and love to others who are lonely in their hard times or just wanting someone to say hello.

You have your own choices. You can be that comma in someone's life too. Be intentional. Can I say that again? Be intentional! Be an instrument for God's voice and His welcoming arms to someone who needs hope.

I feel His smile upon me daily. He has given me loving children, grandchildren and great grandchildren. All of them love and serve Jesus! God has blessed my finances, my relationships, and my health. God has turned my periods of hopelessness into commas with every step, and I'm basking in His goodness now. I'm so thankful. Yes, He has made and continues to make something beautiful out of my life.

He will do the same for you. Let Him. And don't give Him a time limit. Applaud the commas replacing the periods in your life.